A Keepsake of Cats

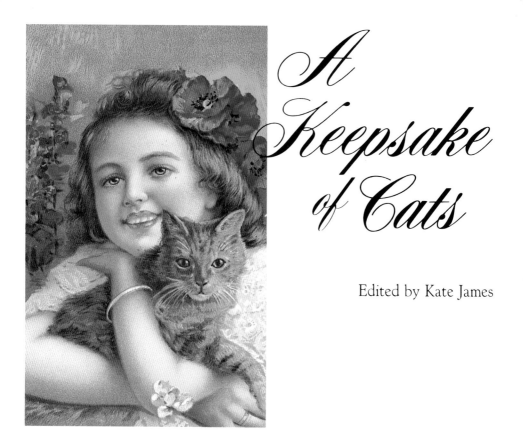

A Keepsake of Cats

Edited by Kate James

Gramercy Books
New York • Avenel, New Jersey

Introduction and Compilation
Copyright © 1992 by Outlet Book Company, Inc.
All rights reserved
First published in 1992 by Gramercy Books
distributed by Outlet Book Company, Inc.,
a Random House Company,
40 Engelhard Avenue
Avenel, New Jersey 07001

Manufactured in Hong Kong

Designed by Melissa Ring

Library of Congress Cataloging-in-Publication Data
A Keepsake of cats.
p.   cm.
ISBN 0-517-07755-8
1. Cats—Literary collections.
PN6071.C3K4   1992
820.8′036—dc20   91-39847   CIP

8 7 6 5 4 3 2 1

Introduction

Cat lovers are more devoted than any other animal lovers, and the creatures upon which we dote know this full well. They seem to regard us as trusted family retainers: We are loved, in our place. A cat can certainly look at a king, as the old proverb goes; the real question is whether a king can look at a cat.

The answer is a qualified yes—only if the look is admiring. The selections in this little anthology should fill the bill: Théophile Gautier, the nineteenth-century French author, takes an appropriately reverential attitude, for example, as does the philosopher Montaigne, quoted here by Isaac Walton. Leigh Hunt's paen to the kitty by the hearth is suitably warm, and President Theodore Roosevelt's letter to his son at school about the new kitten at the White House is proper praise from the highest quarter. Dr. Samuel Johnson, the eighteenth-century author and wit, was so enamored of his cat, Hodge, it annoyed his biographer, James Boswell, no end. But cat lovers fully understand such devotion.

Other contributors to this charming book include such giants of English and American literature as John Keats and Sir Walter Scott, Mark Twain and Henry David Thoreau—as articulate a group of cat fanciers as you'll find anywhere. And any cat could tell you (but probably wouldn't bother) that it takes an impressive group of thinkers to do justice to such a grand subject.

KATE JAMES

New York
1992

TO A CAT

Stately, kindly, lordly friend,
    Condescend
Here to sit by me, and turn
Glorious eyes that smile and burn,
Golden eyes, love's lustrous meed,
On the golden page I read.

All your wondrous wealth of hair
    Dark and fair,
Silken-shaggy, soft and bright
As the clouds and beams of night,
Pays my reverent hand's caress
Back with friendlier gentleness.

Dogs may fawn on all and some
    As they come;
You, a friend of loftier mind,
Answer friends alone in kind!
Just your foot upon my hand
Softly bids it understand.

ALGERNON SWINBURNE

To gain the friendship of a cat is a difficult thing. The cat is a philosophical, methodical, quiet animal, tenacious of his own habits, fond of order and cleanliness, and does not lightly confer his friendship. If you are worthy of his affection, a cat will be your friend but never your slave. He keeps his free will though he loves, and will not do for you what he thinks unreasonable; but if he once gives himself to you, it is with absolute confidence and fidelity of affection. He makes himself the companion of your hours of solitude, melancholy, and toil. He will remain for whole evenings on your knee, uttering a contented purr, happy to be with you. Put him down and he will jump up again with a sort of cooing sound that is a gentle reproach; and sometimes he will sit upon the carpet in front of you looking at you with eyes so melting, so caressing, and so human that they almost frighten you, for it is impossible to believe that a soul is not there.

Théophile Gautier

In a dim corner of my room for longer than my fancy
   thinks
A beautiful and silent Sphinx has watched me through the
   shifting gloom.

Inviolate and immobile she does not rise, she does not stir,
For silver moons are naught to her and naught to her the
   suns that reel.

Red follows gray across the air, the waves of moonlight
   ebb and flow
But with the Dawn she does not go and in the night-time
   she is there.

Dawn follows Dawn and Nights grow old and all the
   while this curious cat
Lies crouching on the Chinese mat with eyes of satin
   rimmed with gold.

OSCAR WILDE

Henriette Ronner.
1902.

A blazing fire, a warm rug, candles lit and curtains drawn, the kettle on for tea, and finally, the cat before you, attracting your attention—it is a scene which everybody likes. The cat purrs, as if it applauded our consideration, and gently moves its tail. What an odd expression of the power to be irritable and the will to be pleased there is in its face, as it looks up at us!

Now she proceeds to clean herself all over, having a just sense of the demands of her elegant person, beginning judiciously with her paws, and fetching amazing tongues at her hind-hips. Anon, she scratches her neck with a foot of rapid delight, leaning her head toward it, and shutting her eyes half to accommodate the action of the skin, and half to enjoy the luxury. She then rewards her paws with a few more touches—look at the action of her head and neck, how pleasing it is, the ears pointed forward, and the neck gently arching to and fro. Finally, she gives a sneeze, and another twist of mouth and whiskers, and then, curling her tail toward her front claws, settles herself on her hind quarters in an attitude of bland meditation.

Leigh Hunt

A home without a cat, and a well-fed, well-petted and properly revered cat, may be a perfect home, perhaps, but how can it prove its title?

Mark Twain

I am the cat of cats. I am
   The everlasting cat!
Cunning, and old, and sleek as jam,
   The everlasting cat!
I hunt the vermin in the night—
   The everlasting cat!
For I see best without the light—
   The everlasting cat!

WILLIAM BRIGHTY RANDS

I never shall forget the indulgence with which he treated Hodge, his cat; for whom he himself used to go out and buy oysters, lest the servants having that trouble should take a dislike to the poor creature. I am, unluckily, one of those who have an antipathy to a cat, so that I am uneasy when in the room with one; and I own, I frequently suffered a good deal from the presence of the same Hodge. I recollect him one day scrambling up Dr. Johnson's breast, apparently with much satisfaction, while my friend, smiling and half-whistling, rubbed his back, and pulled him by the tail; and when I observed he was a fine cat, saying, "Why, yes, Sir, but I have had cats whom I liked better than this," and then, as if perceiving Hodge to be out of countenance, adding, "but he is a very fine cat, a very fine cat indeed."

James Boswell, in his biography
of Dr. Samuel Johnson

HODGE, THE CAT

Burly and big, his books among,
    Good Samuel Johnson sat,
With frowning brows and wig askew,
His snuff-strewn waistcoat far from
    new;
So stern and menacing his air,
    That neither Black Sam, nor the maid
To knock or interrupt him dare;
    Yet close beside him, unafraid,
        Sat Hodge, the cat.

"This participle," the Doctor wrote,
    "The modern scholar cavils at,
But,"—even as he penned the word,
A soft, protesting note was heard;
The Doctor fumbled with his pen,
    The dawning thought took wings and
        flew,
The sound repeated, come again,
    It was a faint, reminding "Mew!"
        From Hodge, the cat.

"Poor Pussy!" said the learned man,
	Giving the glossy fur a pat,
"It is your dinner time, I know,
And—well, perhaps I ought to go;
For if Sam every day were sent
	Off from his work your fish to buy,
Why, men are men, he might resent,
	And starve or kick you on the sly;
		Eh! Hodge, my cat?"

The Dictionary was laid down,
	The Doctor tied his vast cravat,
And down the buzzing street he strode,
Taking an often-trodden road,
And halted at a well-known stall:
	"Fishmonger," spoke the Doctor gruff,
"Give me six oysters, that is all;
	Hodge knows when he has had enough,
		Hodge is my cat."

Then home; puss dined, and while in sleep
	He chased a visionary rat,
His master sat him down again,
Rewrote his page, renibbed his pen;
Each "i" was dotted, each "t" was crossed,
	He labored on for all to read,
Nor deemed that time was waste or lost
	Spent in supplying the small need
		Of Hodge, the cat.

The dear old Doctor! fierce of mien,
	Untidy, arbitrary, fat,
What gentle thought his name enfold!
So generous of his scanty gold.
So quick to love, so hot to scorn,
	Kind to all sufferers under heaven,
A tend'rer despot ne'er was born;
	His big heart held a corner, even
		For Hodge, the cat.

SUSAN COOLIDGE

A Poet's Cat, sedate and grave
As poet well could wish to have,
Was much addicted to inquire
For nooks to which she might retire,
And where, secure as mouse in chink,
She might repose, or sit and think.
I know not where she caught the trick—
Nature perhaps herself had cast her
In such a mold *philosophique*,
Or else she learn'd it of her Master.
Sometimes ascending, debonnair,
An apple tree, or lofty pear,
Lodg'd with convenience in the fork,
She watch'd the gard'ner at his work;
Sometimes her ease and solace sought
In an old empty wat'ring pot,
There wanting nothing, save a fan,
To seem some nymph in her sedan
Apparell'd in exactest sort,
And ready to be borne to court.

WILLIAM COWPER

Tom Quartz is certainly the cunningest kitten I have ever seen. He is always playing pranks on Jack and I get very nervous lest Jack should grow too irritated. The other evening they were both in the library—Jack sleeping before the fire—Tom Quartz scampering about, an exceedingly playful little creature—which is about what he is. He would race across the floor, then jump upon the curtain or play with the tassel. Suddenly he spied Jack and galloped up to him. Jack, looking exceedingly sullen and shame-faced, jumped out of the way and got upon the sofa and around the table, and Tom Quartz instantly jumped upon him again. Jack suddenly shifted to the other sofa, where Tom Quartz again went after him. Then Jack started for the door, while Tom made a rapid turn under the sofa and around the table and just as Jack reached the door leaped on his hindquarters. Jack bounded forward and away and the two went tandem out of the room—Jack not co-operating at all; and about five minutes afterwards Tom Quartz stalked solemnly back.

President Theodore Roosevelt in a letter
to his little son, Kermit, who had just
returned to school in January of 1903

JESSIE WILLCOX SMITH.

I like little Pussy,
    Her coat is so warm;
And if I don't hurt her
    She'll do me no harm.
So I'll not pull her tail,
    Nor drive her away,
But Pussy and I
    Very gentle will play;
She shall sit by my side,
    And I'll give her some food;
And she'll love me because
    I am gentle and good.
I'll pat little Pussy,
    And then she will purr.
And thus show her thanks
    For my kindness to her;
I'll not pinch her ears.
    Nor tread on her paw,
Lest I should provoke her
    To use her sharp claw;
I never will vex her,
    Nor make her displeased,
For Pussy can't bear
    To be worried or teased.

JANE TAYLOR

*I*n the great Zoological Gardens . . . the boon companion of the colossal elephant was a common cat! This cat had a fashion of climbing up the elephant's hind legs and roosting on his back. She would sit up there, with her paws curved under her breast, and sleep in the sun half the afternoon. It used to annoy the elephant at first, and he would reach up and take her down, but she would go aft and climb up again. She persisted until she finally conquered the elephant's prejudices, and now they are inseparable friends. The cat plays about her comrade's forefeet or his trunk often, until dogs approach, and then she goes aloft out of danger. The elephant has annihilated several dogs lately that pressed his companion too closely.

From The Innocents Abroad *by Mark Twain,*
about the zoo in Marseille

Thou hast seen Atossa sage
Sit for hours beside thy cage;
Thou wouldst chirp, thou foolish bird,
Flutter, chirp—she never stirr'd!
What were now these toys to her?
Down she sank amid her fur;
Eyed thee with a soul resign'd—
And thou deemedst cats were kind!
—Cruel, but composed and bland,
Dumb, inscrutable and grand,
So Tiberius might have sat,
Had Tiberius been a cat.

MATTHEW ARNOLD

The way Dinah washed her children's faces was this: first she held the poor thing down by its ears with one paw, and then with the other paw she rubbed its face all over, the wrong way, beginning at the nose: and just now, as I said, she was hard at work on the white kitten, which was lying quite still and trying to purr—no doubt feeling that it was all meant for its good.

But the black kitten had been finished with earlier in the afternoon, and so, while Alice was sitting curled up in a corner of the great armchair, half talking to herself and half asleep, the kitten had been having a grand game of romps with the ball of worsted Alice had been trying to wind up, and had been rolling it up and down till it had all come undone again; and there it was, spread over the hearth-rug, all knots and tangles, with the kitten running after its own tail in the middle.

"Oh, you wicked little thing!" cried Alice, catching up the kitten, and giving it a little kiss to make it understand that it was in disgrace. "Really, Dinah ought to have taught you better manners! You ought, Dinah, you know you ought!"

From Through the Looking Glass *by Lewis Carroll*

THE CAT

Dear creature by the fire a-purr,
   Strange idol, eminently bland,
Miraculous puss! As o'er your fur
   I trail a negligible hand,

And gaze into your gazing eyes,
   And wonder in a demi-dream
What mystery is it that lies
   Behind those slits that glare and gleam,

An exquisite enchantment falls
   About the portals of my sense;
Meandering through enormous halls
   I breathe luxurious frankincense,

An ampler air, a warmer June
   Enfold me, and my wandering eye
Salutes a more imperial moon
   Throned in a more resplendent sky

Than ever knew this northern shore.
　　Oh, strange! For you are with me too,
And I who am a cat once more
　　Follow the woman that was you.

With tail erect and pompous march,
　　The proudest puss that ever trod,
Through many a grove, 'neath many an arch,
　　Impenetrable as a god.

LYTTON STRACHEY

As the learned and ingenious Montaigne says . . . "When my cat and I entertain each other with mutual apish tricks, as playing with a garter, who knows but that I make my cat more sport than she makes me? Shall I conclude her to be simple, that has her time to begin or refuse to play as freely as I myself have? Nay, who knows but that it is a defect of my not understanding her language (for doubtless cats talk and reason with one another), that we agree no better? And who knows but that she pities me for being no wiser than to play with her, and laughs and censures my folly for making sport for her, when we two play together."

From The Compleat Angler *by Izaak Walton*

Bentham was very fond of animals, particularly "pussies," as he called them, when they had domestic virtues, but he had no particular affection for the common race of cats. He had one, however, of which he used to boast that he had "made a man of him," and whom he was wont to invite to eat macaroni at his own table. This puss got knighted, and rejoiced in the name of Sir John Langbourne. In his early days he was a frisky, inconsiderate, and, to say the truth, somewhat profligate gentleman; and had, according to the report of his patron, the habit of seducing light and giddy young ladies, of his own race, into the garden of Queen's Square Place: but tired at last, like Solomon, of pleasures and vanities, he became sedate and thoughtful—took to the church, laid down his knightly title, and was installed as the Reverend John Langbourne. He gradually obtained a great reputation for sanctity and learning, and a Doctor's degree was conferred upon him. When I knew him, in his declining days, he bore no other name than the Reverend Doctor John Langbourne: and he was alike conspicuous for his gravity and philosophy.

John Bowring, writing about the cat of his friend Jeremy Bentham, the nineteenth-century English philosopher and creator of Utilitarianism.

Cat! who hast pass'd thy grand climacteric,
  How many mice and rats hast in thy days
  Destroy'd?—How many tit bits stolen? Gaze
With those bright languid segments green, and prick
Those velvet ears—but pr'ythee do not stick
  Thy latent talons in me—and upraise
  Thy gentle mew—and tell me all thy frays
Of fish and mice, and rats and tender chick.
Nay, look not down, nor lick thy dainty wrists—
  For all the wheezy asthma,—and for all
Thy tail's tip is nick'd off—and though the fists
  Of many a maid have given thee many a maul,
Still is that fur as soft as when the lists
  In youth thou enter'dst on glass-bottled wall.

JOHN KEATS

Min caught a mouse, and was playing with it in the yard. It had got away from her once or twice and she had caught it again, and now it was stealing off again, as she was complacently watching it with her paws tucked under her, when her friend, Riorden, a stout cock, stepped up inquisitively, looked down at the mouse with one eye, turning its head, then picked it up by the tail, gave it two or three whacks on the ground, and giving it a dexterous toss in the air, caught the mouse in its open mouth. It went, head foremost and alive, down Riorden's capacious throat in the twinkling of an eye, never again to be seen in this world; Min all the while, with paws comfortably tucked under her, looking on unconcerned. What did one mouse matter, more or less, to her? The cock walked off amid the currant-bushes, stretched his neck up and gulped once or twice, and the deed was accomplished. Then he crowed lustily in celebration of the exploit. It might be set down among the *Gesta gallorum*. There were several human witnesses. It is a question whether Min ever understood where that mouse went to. She sits composedly sentinel, with paws tucked under her, a good part of her days at present, by some ridiculous little hole, the possible entry of a mouse.

Henry David Thoreau

*F*or I will consider my Cat Jeoffry,
For he is the servant of the Living God duly and
daily serving Him.
For at the first glance of the glory of God in the
East he worships in his way.
For is this done by wreathing his body seven times
round with elegant quickness.
For then he leaps up to catch the musk, which is the
blessing of God upon his prayer.
For he rolls upon prank to work it in.

For having done duty and received blessing he
    begins to consider himself.
For this he performs in ten degrees.
For first he looks upon his fore-paws to see if they
    are clean.
For secondly he kicks up behind to clear away
    there.
For thirdly he works it upon stretch with the fore-
    paws extended.
For fourthly he sharpens his paws by wood.
For fifthly he washes himself.
For sixthly he rolls upon wash.
For seventhly he fleas himself, that he may not be
    interrupted upon the beat.
For eighthly he rubs himself against a post.
For ninthly he looks up for his instructions.
For tenthly he goes in quest of food.
For having consider'd God and himself he will
    consider his neighbor.

From "Jubilate Agno" by Christopher Smart,
an eighteenth-century poet who was
confined to an insane asylum in London
with only his cat, Jeoffry, for company

TO MY CAT

*H*alf loving-kindliness, and half disdain,
Thou comest to my call serenely suave,
With humming speech and gracious gestures grave,
In salutation courtly and urbane:
Yet must I humble me thy grace to gain—
For wiles may win thee, but no arts enslave,
And nowhere gladly thou abidest save
Where naught disturbs the concord of thy reign.
Sphinx of my quiet hearth! who deignst to dwell,
Friend of my toil, companion of mine ease,
Thine is the lore of Rā and Rameses;
That men forget dost thou remember well,
Beholden still in blinking reveries,
With somber sea-green eyes inscrutable.

ROSAMUND MARRIOTT WATSON

. . . . Three proper men out of five will always throw things at a Cat whenever they meet him, and all proper Dogs will chase him up a tree. But the Cat keeps his side of the bargain too. He will kill Mice and he will be kind to Babies when he is in the house, as long as they do not pull his tail too hard. But when he has done that, and between times, he is the Cat that walks by himself and all places are alike to him, and if you look out at nights you can see him waving his wild tail and walking by his wild lone—just the same as before.

From "The Cat That Walked by Himself"
by Rudyard Kipling

Cats are a mysterious kind of folk.

There is more passing in their minds

than we are aware of.

Sir Walter Scott

ODE ON THE DEATH OF A FAVORITE CAT DROWNED IN A TUB OF GOLD FISHES

'Twas on a lofty vase's side
Where China's gayest art had dyed
  The azure flowers, that blow;
Demurest of the tabby kind,
The pensive Selima, reclined,
  Gazed on the lake below.

Her conscious tail her joy declared;
The fair round face, the snowy beard,
   The velvet of her paws,
Her coat, that with the tortoise vies,
Her ears of jet, and emerald eyes,
   She saw; and purr'd applause.

Still had she gazed; but 'midst the tide
Two angel forms were seen to glide,
   The genii of the stream:
Their scaly armor's Tyrian hue
Through richest purple to the view
   Betray'd a golden gleam.

The hapless nymph with wonder saw:
A whisker first, and then a claw,
   With many an ardent wish,
She stretch'd, in vain, to reach the prize.
What female heart can gold despise?
   What cat's averse to fish?

Presumptuous maid! with looks intent
Again she stretch'd, again she bent,
   Nor knew the gulf between.
(Malignant Fate sat by, and smiled)
The slipp'ry verge her feet beguiled,
   She tumbled headlong in.

Eight times emerging from the flood
She mew'd to ev'ry wat'ry God,
   Some speedy aid to send.
No Dolphin came, no Nereid stirr'd:
Nor cruel Tom, nor Susan heard.
   A fav'rite has no friend!

From hence, ye beauties, undeceived,
Know, one false step is ne'er retrieved,
   And be with caution bold.
Not all that tempts your wand'ring eyes
And heedless hearts is lawful prize;
   Nor all that glitters, gold.

THOMAS GRAY

ELEGY

Bathsheba: To whom none ever said scat,
No worthier cat
Ever sat on a mat
Or caught a rat:
Requies-cat.

JOHN GREENLEAF WHITTIER

No. Heaven will not ever Heaven be

Unless my cats are there to welcome me.

Author Unknown